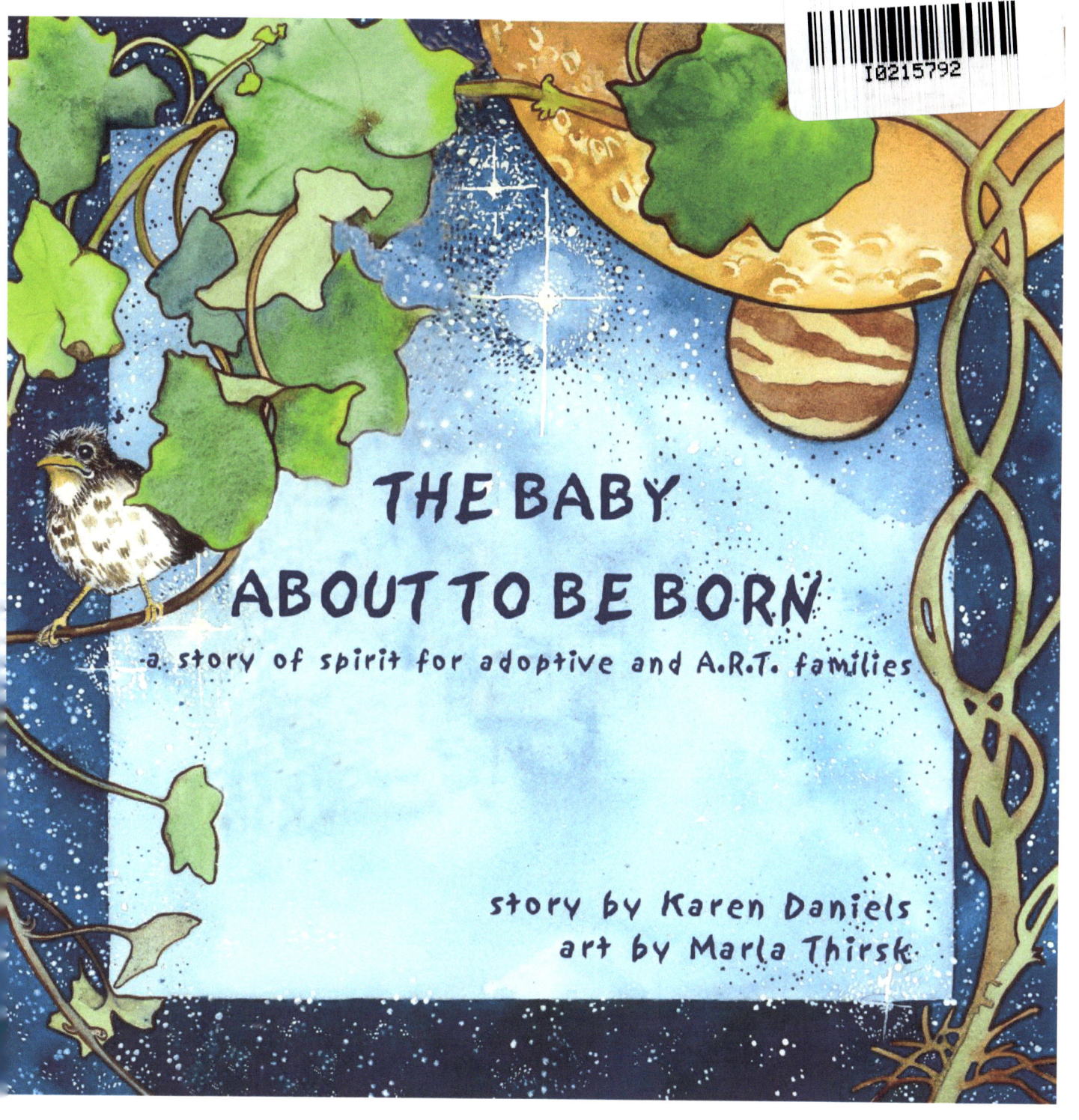

Once upon all time,
in the land of the Soon-To-Be-Born,
there was a little spirit
named Baybo.

Baybo was about to be born.

And he knew when he was born he wanted to be a little boy.

Baybo attended Earth planning classes with other little spirits in the land of Stobb, (which is what the land of the Soon-To-Be-Born is called).

All the spirits in the class were brightly colored souls, with blues and greens and reds and grays and all the colors that are imagined.

Baybo was made of many colors too, and right across his front he had a bright blaze of gold.

He was the only one in his class like this.

One day Baybo was floating in life-planning class and watching as his classmates laughed and planned and talked about the kind of parents they wanted.

One of them named Terpi turned to Baybo and said, "Baybo, come over here and tell us about the parents you want."

"I don't know who I want my parents to be." Baybo sighed and stayed where he was in the back of the room.

"If you don't know who to pick, how can you become someone's child?" a spirit with lots of orange and green asked.

"I'm not sure." Baybo's colors dulled.

So Baybo, the spirit with the gold streak, who wanted very much to be someone's little boy, watched quietly as all the spirits around him finished up their lessons and picked their parents.

Still Baybo couldn't make up his mind.

While the other spirits played their last games together, and laughed, and planned, and joked, and dreamed their dreams...

Baybo wondered what he was going to do.

The day came when the first of Baybo's classmates winked out of Stobb. One moment she was there, the next she was gone.

Gone to become a little girl named Gloria and live her dreams on Earth.

Fornax, the teacher of the class, was a knowing soul. When Gloria left to go to Earth, Fornax paused in the lesson and said, "Let us rejoice. Another life is about to be born on Earth."

A hum filled the air and there was joy.

And then it was back to the lessons and dreaming their dreams.

Time passed and every day the same thing happened. Class would begin; spirits would wink out to be born; lessons would go on.

In no time at all there were very few left in the class.

Baybo, the little spirit with the gold streak, worried he would be left in the land of the Soon-To-Be-Born forever and never get to be anyone's little boy.

This made him so sad.

 Soon there were only three other spirits left in Baybo's class...

then only two others...

 then one.

And finally, the other spirit was gone and Baybo was all alone.

Fornax glimmered and shimmered and sat down next to the boy who wanted to be born and asked, "Do you know yet who you want to be born to?"

"No." Baybo shook with unhappiness then spoke what was in his heart. "I want to do something really special. Can you help me?"

The teacher thought, colors swirling. "Yes, I think I can. Come with me."

Fornax led Baybo to the most beautiful room he'd ever seen. There were colors of rainbows from all worlds, and the most glorious music.

Yet there was a big sadness in the room, too.

"What is this place?" Baybo asked. "It's so beautiful and so sad."

"This is the room that holds the love and wishes of parents who long for children but have not yet been able to have them."

"Wow." Baybo looked at the room with wonder.

Fornax continued talking.

"And others here must search the world over for their child—a child who is born to someone else but really belongs with them. When they find their child, they adopt them into their family."

Baybo sighed, wanting to find his own family.

"The babies and parents must be happy to be together after waiting so long."

"Yes." Fornax answered. "They are very happy."

Baybo took a deep breath. "All these parents must really want a child."

"More than anything." Fornax nodded. "The people with dreams in this room wish for children with their hearts and souls and faith."

Fornax hugged Baybo and said,

"We only allow very special little spirits to go to these people."

Little Baybo, the soon-to-be-boy, smiled in a way he'd never smiled before. "I want to go to someone who has wishes in this room. Am I special enough?"

"Yes. You are. And no parents will love you more than these. All you have to do is figure out the real reason spirits are born on Earth. Look at yourself and you will see."

Baybo looked down at his colors. After a moment his eyes grew wide. "I think I know!" Baybo felt as if he were about to burst. "The answer is in the gold streak!"

"What is it?" Fornax smiled.

"It's love, isn't it?" The little spirit danced.

Fornax nodded. "Yes. Love in its purest form."

Baybo's colors swirled and brightened and the gold streak blazed. He looked around the room and found what he'd been longing for. "My parents are here. Now I know who I want them to be."

With those last words Baybo started to fade and Fornax waved good-bye.

And so, the little spirit named Baybo was born on Earth, where he became a very special child, indeed.

The author and artist of this book have each utilized in-vitro fertilization in their pursuit of motherhood.
The story and art are born from this journey.

The Author: Karen Daniels

Karen is the mother of 3 children created through IVF, founder of Zencopy.com, a blog conversation about writing, creativity, and authentic success. She is the author of numerous books listed on the following page.
Learn more about Karen and her writing at karendaniels.com.

The Artist: Marla Thirsk

The original full color artwork featured in this print version of "The Baby About to be Born" was created by Marla Thirsk, a long time resident of a remote coastal town on Vancouver Island, Canada.
Learn more about Marla and see her art at marlathirsk.com.

Karen Daniels' Books

1. The Baby About to Be Born: A story of spirit for families created with in-vitro fertilization and adoption.

2. In-vitro Fertilization: The Ultimate Reality Game. A true tale of what it's really like to go through IVF. Listen to a radio interview about this book at ivfcreation.com.
Get print version of IVF book at: **https://www.createspace.com/3516461** and use this secret 15% off code: 5JSHH23L.
Get the Kindle version at: **http://www.amazon.com/dp/B004LROPMC.**

3. Your Creativity: From Ordinary to Extraordinary, on print and Kindle
Boost your creativity and live the life you want.

4. Fiction: The Zaddack Tales Trilogy. Special 10th anniversary release –
Dancing Suns, Mentor's Lair, and Mindspark. Easy-reading adventures in spiritual science fiction. Also available as a Kindle version of the complete trilogy.

All rights reserved. Published by karendaniels.com.
No part of this publication may be reproduced or stored in a retrieval system,
or transmitted in any form or by any means, electronic, mechanical, photocopying, recording, or otherwise,
without written permission.

Story copyright © Karen Daniels ☼
Illustrations copyright © Marla Thirsk ☼

Daniels, Karen, The Boy About to be Born, paintings by Marla Thirsk

ISBN-13:
978-0615469539

ISBN-10:
0615469531

www.ingramcontent.com/pod-product-compliance
Lightning Source LLC
Chambersburg PA
CBHW040027050426
42453CB00002B/29